The Me That I Found

Devanie Sether

BookLeat
Publishing

India | USA | UK

Presentation by *BookLeaf Publishing*

Web: www.bookleafpub.com

E-mail: info@bookleafpub.com

ISBN: 9789360944155

First edition 2024

For every version of me that had the strength to endure and survive.

ACKNOWLEDGEMENT

Denice, my mom, is the mastermind behind my name, Devanie. From the Irish name Devan, meaning "Poet." Thank you for being the first and most significant influence on my path as a writer.

Dustin, my brother, plays numerous roles in my life - my editor, publicist, agent, hype man, etc. Thank you for every meeting, emergency hype sesh, phone call and push to get back into the ring. Glad I have you in my corner!

Danene, my sister. Through my darkest times, you are a source of light. My cherished lifeline and source of unwavering support that I hold dear in my heart.

Emily, my sister-in-law. Your open heart and listening ear have been a constant refuge, especially during my moments of uncertainty. I appreciate your encouragement and support so much.

My Cheerleaders! You know who you are! My community of people is the driving force that propels me forward! I am truly grateful for each and every one of you!

The BookLeaf Publishing Team! Your collective efforts have not only provided me with an incredible opportunity but have also been instrumental in bringing my words to life.

PREFACE

Throughout my life, words have been my lifeline; offering comfort in times of solitude, guidance when I needed direction, and a powerful tool for expressing myself. In times when the weight of the world felt unbearable, I discovered solace within the embrace of sentences, paragraphs, and verses.

Being able to express myself through writing became my refuge amidst the storm of what felt like a seemingly insurmountable situation. This book has become a profound outlet for me, offering a unique space to unveil experiences that have long lingered unspoken within me. Through its pages, I sought not just to recount my journey but to intricately weave my narrative that invites healing and celebrates the resilient woman I've evolved into.

In the face of any hardship, the indomitable spirit and unwavering courage can fuel an unstoppable journey of survival!

Anchor to my Cloud

He was my anchor, holding me in place.
As a dreamer, I was a cloud.
I tended to drift away.

The chain linking us together was relaxed,
allowing for space and respect.
But as the anchor beneath the surface
weathered its own storms,
that chain became taut,
not allowing for growth.

The chain tightens,
pulling me away from my heavenly home,
closer to the sea,
and into his idea of safety.

Held just underneath the surface of the water.
Able to peer up to the home I once loved.
Able to gaze beneath me into
the dark stormy waters that I dread.

The storm inside rages on,
suffocation increases with every move I make.
Allow it to take over, there's no use in fighting.
This is your life now, in the deep,
dark waters of the sea.

My Friend Loneliness

In the quiet of my soul,
you've been a constant companion.
Please stay.

In the depths of my heart,
you've comforted me in my darkest times.
Continue to hold me close.

In the secrets I cannot say,
you've heard all of them.
Keep them next to your chest.

For the tears that no one sees,
you've wiped them all away.
You've become my steadfast friend.

Your Shadow

He is lurking again, rearing his ugly head.
He dodges in and out of the dark places,
wreaking havoc with my mind's quiet spaces.

He is changing shape again, adapting your view.
Telling stories of what could be,
even though it's not what you want with me.

He is brooding again, sitting in his own torture.
Whispering his dark thoughts into my ear,
casting clouds of fear.

He is prowling again, silently stalking me.
Looking intently to devour me,
while my back is turned.

Beneath My Smile

In a hidden world resides a realm
of unspoken narratives.
Every curve of my lip is a veil,
concealing the secrets that dwell within.

The sparkle in my eyes, a shimmering mirage,
masks the echoes of my pain and tears.
Behind my expressions are the untold stories,
the silent struggles etched into the lines
that cradles my smile.

A symphony of emotions plays softly,
an intricate dance between
the visible and the concealed.
The true depth of my existence unfurls
beneath the guise of a fleeting smile.

Metal Heart

5

Made up of circuits and steel, he stands,
A creation of precision, built by unknown hands.
Lack of emotion, a flaw is revealed,
Dead eyes gaze, full of pain unhealed.

A cold heart beats within this mechanical frame,
No warmth, no empathy, no flicker of flame.
Yet in his stoic silence, a strange allure,
A creation of steel, a facade so pure.

No joy, no sorrow, no laughter, no tears,
A robotic existence, yet full of human fears.
In the stillness of circuits, a tale unfolds,
Of a creation unfeeling, love he withholds.

Chasing a Mirage

When weariness of the world takes its toll,
Just slip away, into the dreams that console.
A realm where reality takes a backseat,
And the weight on your mind, dreams discreet.

In this sanctuary, fantasies unfold,
The main character, a story to be told.
Dreams, sometimes haunting, sometimes bright,
Taking us on flights through the night.

As slumber embraces, a nocturnal dive,
In the realm of shut eyes, tales come alive.
A world of nothing, yet filled with disguise,
In the silent realm where imagination lies.

Deadly End

In the glass she peers, a reflection so true,
A woman in solitude, fear in her view.
Black and blue, she wears pain like a cloak,
Swallowed by shadows,
a heart engulfed in smoke.

A burden heavy, on her chest it does rest,
An unforgettable ache, pounding in her breast.
She cannot go on, with this weight so profound,
Falling into the abyss,
silence, the only sound.

In the mirror's gaze, she meets her own stare,
A blade in hand, a moment to dare.
Eyes closed tight, she raises the knife,
A slash in the darkness,
surrendering to strife.

Silent screams within, no voice to shout,
Dry tears, a heartache that's drowned out.
On the cold floor, in a crimson pool she lay,
Waiting for darkness
to carry her away.

The shadow's embrace, as the night is near,

A tragic tale whispered, only for hearts to hear.
In the stillness, she crumples, a soul worn thin,
A dance with the dark,
where no light could win.

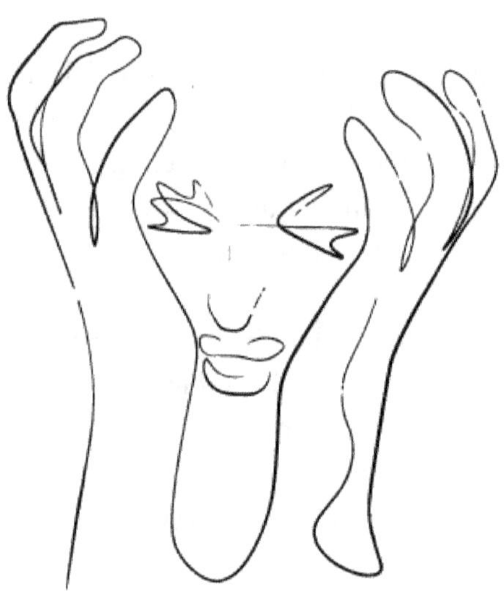

Confined in Fear

Words that linger, hovering in the air,
Feelings concealed, lies of a silent affair.
In my eyes, a reflection of fear you find,
On my face, the traces of a heart, confined.

Memories linger, in shadows they cascade.
Lines of the past, etched with "I am afraid,"
Yesterday lingers, the pain doesn't fade,
Nothing lasts forever, each moment, a trade.

In my cage of fear, where shadows play,
The heart whispers, longing for the light of day.
Today is new, a chance to break fears' plight,
By unveiling this chapter, yesterday took flight.

Silent No More

In the caverns of silence, where secrets confide,
A muted existence, where truths subside.
In the whispers of his betrayal, a haunting song,
I clung to illusions, ignoring what was wrong.

Whispered doubt becomes a part of my reality,
All of his denial confuses my validity.
Trapped in a spider web of self-hatred,
Because of the lies he has narrated.

Unspeakable wounds
have been inflicted upon me,
Hidden scars underneath
the surface no one can see.

I will no longer keep his secrets,
I am breaking my silence.
The deepest parts of him are revealed,
exposed by my defiance.

The Fear

In the height of my struggles,
tears refuse to fall.

Laughter eludes me,
a distant echo in the hall.

A stolen voice,
trapped in the shadows, stifles my scream.

Tripping over my own feet, I falter,
unable to run free.

The ache within, too intense to bear,
leaves me numb, unable to feel.

Ghost

Disappear quickly, vanish into thin air.
Leaving behind what you expected me to be.

My unspoken departure screamed volumes,
This courageous step into the unknown.

Dissolving like whispers that are
washed away by the rain,
Fading into the shadows of my own liberation.

Clarity

Opened wide.
Closed tight.

Eyes darting from left to right.
Not knowing where to look,
what to see,
who to be?

Once you see the light,
you turn away from the dark.
Once you realize the truth,
you no longer believe the lies.

From the Void

Seeds that were planted have withered,
With neglect comes loss.
No sunshine or rain to nurture the ground
Grief and pain, buried underneath.

Then one day the earth awoke
Shattering ground, breaking worlds apart
Uneven and rocky, no longer steadfast
those once-forgotten seeds unfurled.

Closer to the surface they became
Where they could feel sunshine
and be healed by rain.

Amidst the garden of wounds, petals arise
embracing the scars from the life endured
with resilient blooms, sprouting seeds grow
In the valley of my broken heart.

Beacons of Light

In the stillness of the night,
they emerge,
silent guides that pierce the darkness.

With hopeful glimmers they light the path I take,
leading me towards the realm of
new beginnings.

As my journey unfolds,
shadows of the past give way
To the promise of a brighter, uncharted future.

My celestial lanterns burn bright from
deep beneath,
urging me with each step forward.

Moving further away from what used to be
Into the possibility of what awaits on the other
side of darkness.

Every One of Me

In the glassy lake I see
the little girl who used to believe.
Whose dreams spanned far and wide
Casts a glow of who I was inside.

Through the echoing wind I hear
Songs of the young woman who showed no fear.
Her bravery was her greatest value.
And to myself, I stayed true.

Hiding behind the dark within,
A mere shadow of the person I once had been.
A shell navigating life's turbulent tide,
Survival, the sole purpose, emotions set aside.

Grasping me by the hand,
is the woman that I am.
Together we have been through it all,
I know I can count on myself when I fall.

There is one I have yet to meet,
Is the one that I will be.
Wise, older and demonstrating grace,
Even with those extra smile lines on my face.

While at times I may have lost my way
There has been one that has always stayed.
In this story of who I have been, who I was,
who I am and will be,
The constant, always and forever is, Me.

To Find Me...

Across the vast ocean,
with creatures untamed,
I'll seek where I belong,
where my essence is named.

Scaling each mountain,
beneath every tree's shade,
In pursuit of my place,
where authenticity is laid.

Through distances traveled,
lands far and wide,
Conversing with each soul,
extending a guide.

Seeking where I fit,
where I can simply be.
Extending a hand to all,
fostering unity.

In every season's grasp,
summer, winter, fall, and spring,
Exploring life's tapestry,
on every wing.

Surveying each place,
and many, many more,

Discovering my purpose,
bringing joy to the core.

Yet, amid the journey,
a realization profound,
In my heart's reflection,
my true self is found.

No need for exhaustive quest
or endless roam.
For I am home,
in the sanctuary of my own.

The Heart of Your Soul

In the depths where feelings reside,
Favorite things in its chambers hide.
A spirit's haven, where rest is found,
The beginning of love, where hate is drowned.

Poisonous shadows may attempt their reign,
Yet goodness triumphs, breaking the chain.
The constant you count on, in life's intricate plot,
Where hopes can bloom, and patience is sought.

A key to happiness, a doorway to sadness,
A guide through darkness, a beacon in gladness.
The threshold to sorrow, the gateway to mirth,
The keeper of night, the passage of Earth.

Believe it or not, in its ethereal scroll,
Your entire essence rests, the heart of your soul.

Step Into Power

Strength in your footsteps,
echoes of grace,
Leaving behind shadows,
embracing a new space.
In the garden of dreams,
each bloom unfolds,
A story of healing,
the future foretold.

Witness the sunrise
in your laughter's presence.
Dancing with joy,
adorned with newfound essence.
Discovering treasures
within your own core.
A self-love so deep,
like never before.

Look at you,
a beacon, a guiding source.
Navigating storms,
an emerging force.
Embracing the whispers
of wind and of sea,
A melody of freedom,

a soul unchained and free.

In the reflection of mirrors,
a vision so clear,
The future you smiles,
conquering fear.
The scars that remain,
now tell a tale,
Of resilience and triumph,
a ship that set sail.